It Is My Time: The Anthology of Me

Gnatee Doe

While the author has made every effort to provide accurate contact information at the time of publication, neither the publisher nor the author assumes any responsibility for errors, or for changes that occur after publication. Further, the publisher does not have any control over and does not assume any responsibility for author or third-party websites or their content.

The author uses words or language that are considered profane, vulgar, or offensive by some readers.

Printed in the United States of America

First Printing, 2017

ISBN-13: 978-0998988900
ISBN-10: 0998988901
Library of Congress Control Number: 2017944995

Convexed Cognitive Publications
1479 Shady Pl #4108
Daytona Beach, FL 32114
convexedcognition@gmail.com

A copy of this book may be purchased on Amazon.com

Cover Photograph by Selina Puentes
Author Photograph by Selina Puentes

Introduction

This book chronicles the beginning of a journey, on a path to creative writing. In sharing all of my poetry from age 10 to 24, I open you up to a world of vulnerability, maturation, acceptance, and evolution.

I was apprehensive at first, fearing that my initial work wouldn't be worth including in my anthology. After years of rediscovering myself and reinvigorating my passion for writing, I realized that every word, every concept, and every title that I have penned, was crucial to making me who I have become.

From the eyes of a 10-year-old eighth grade student, to the curiosity of a 16-year-old college freshman, concluding with the self-reflection of a father and husband by age 20; I give you a portion of my life through rhyme, verse, and metaphor.

Contents

Early Years

Seed of Sorrow   8

Tale of Sorrow and Death   9

Endless Love   10

Divine Spirit   11

Why   12

Rose of Passion   13

Starlight Fever   14

Rage   15

A Son Knows His Moher's Pain   17

A Window in the Ghetto   20

No Way Out   21

Beautiful Woman   22

Woman- The Greatest Gift   23

It's Crazy   25

I'm Tired   26

Help   28

So Many Questions not Enough Answers   30

Later Years and Collegiate Life

Slain by Beauty   32

Trinity of 4   33

Mi Amor   34

Made Whole   36

A Good Man   37

Complex yet Simple   38

Emphatic Pleasures   40

One Day Imma have to Tell Her   42

Affinity   43

She's Different   44

Realizing She's No Longer Here   45

Art Thou Thy Brother's Keeper   47

Poetic Expression   51

His Story   53

THIS LOCK   that key   56

JADYN   57

Stand Still   59

One   61

She is Not Just Any She   63

If It Were Not For The Thin   64

Cherish Her   66

Sleepwalking   67

EARLY ADOLESCENT YEARS

The age of ten was my first step into the world of writing. My words were infused with emotion, without a real focus on style or format. It was a journey into a realm of expressing myself, as best I knew how…

Seed of Sorrow

There is one thing in my life,
I would never want to borrow.
That one thing is full of death and strife;
Seed of sorrow.

Why have you taken this soul away from me?
Is there anything that would become of me?
Please, please, seed of sorrow—
Bring this soul back to me tomorrow.

Tale of Sorrow and Death

Hearts crash along the silent river,
they cry out for need.
Looking for love from each other,
the reaps and sows of their love they needed to mead.

Here in the light,
they sit there and shatter;
down at the river in tears.
No hope for them as their minds clutter,
and now they see all of their fears.

Then in the end altogether,
the worst comes together,
they end their lives on the scene.
Now we see how life can be mean.

Endless Love

Love throughout the shining star.
Love that goes beyond and far.
Endless love throughout the night.
Endless love that brings in the light.

Love that seeks a lonely heart.
Love that is so near but far apart.
Knowing what it has to do,
Is bring together me and you.

Divine Spirit

Who has blessed you till this day?
Would you be mine?
Who has made you this way—
To look so lovely and divine?

Your beauty shines in the light.
In every star throughout the night.
When I look into your eyes, I see a dazzling brown.
And knowing how beautiful you are,
you would never frown.

When you are deceased
and life passes on;
Your beauty will never decrease,
for it will tag along.

Your soul will reign forever.
No person will ever say never...
To the joy that you will bring,
when your blessed soul starts to sing.

Why

Why has love deceived me this way?
Why has love given me someone, who
will leave me day after day?

Why has love given me all this pain?
Why has love brought down the rain?
Let it be or it shall be done,
that I do not deserve the love of anyone.

Rose of Passion

Rose of passion,
Rose of love,
Rose that falls from the heavens above.

Rose that shines as bright as the moonlight.
Rose that brings in the illustrious red light.
Rose the color of our blood;
That gives you your beauty—
Face of a flower bud.

Rose of passion,
Rose from above,
It is the one that gives you,
The grace and light of love.

Starlight Fever

In the wake of night,
in the dawn of light—
waiting for the day to be through.
And sitting on my door steps thinking,
About the love I could share with you.

Laying there looking at the shining star.
Wondering where you are...
I just want you to know,
How I love you so.

Starlight fever throughout the night.
Starlight fever that brings in the light.
Let the wings of love take us on a beautiful flight;
So that I can hold you through the night.

Rage

I am angry,
And I don't know why.
I am angry,
With every moment that passes by.
I am angry,
With all the things that are taken away.
I am angry,
With every moment of everyday.
When I get like this,
I can't control it.
Sometimes I wanna scream,
Because I can't stand it.
At any moment,
Any little thing can tick me off;
For the simple fact—
That I cannot control my thoughts.
Maybe I need to be myself…
Maybe not.
But I need to do something
To move the clock.
At times I have to cry,
To release the things that are on my mind.
… I wish, I could get krump,
To release the pain and disappointment
In my life.
I'm tired,
Of the situations and circumstances
That I'm in.
But God's favorites get it the worse…
I'm tired,
Of having all of these emotions

Held within—
At times, it seems
That nothing can go my way.
The frustration of the circumstance
Causes dismay.
It's tiring,
When you constantly have to battle
With your thoughts;
Constantly fighting a battle,
That shouldn't have to be fought.

A Son Knows His Mother's Pain

Life is something so fragile.
A child is born,
A child is lost,
A mother is torn,
Thinking it was her fault.

Maybe—she feels—
She let go too soon.
Tired of the arguing,
Tired of the pain,
Tired of the complaining,
Tired of the circumstances being the same.

She realizes he's growing old…
Yet she still wants him to remain young.
Though he disregards everything he's told,
She still loves her son.

They clash—
Because they're one in the same.
Five children,
But of a different name.
He loves his mother,
But feels suppressed.
At any moment he blows up,
Releasing everything off his chest.

He knows it's because
Of the things he went through.
But that is no excuse—
And he doesn't use it.

Wears his emotions on his sleeve,
But don't misconstrue it.

A "good guy",
As proclaimed by others.
Maybe it's his downfall…
Because he doesn't want to treat
A female he likes, like he's seen his mother.

But he can't help it.
He loves his father,
But at the same time doesn't give a shit.
And it's for the simple fact,
That he can't stand his father's ways.
Seeing his mother cry, complain,
And suffer every day.

It's hard to hear his mother
Tell him of the hurt and pain.
Wishing he could do something
To make her feel happy…
To bring about change.

But it doesn't work—
And with that failure,
The anger mounts.
He regurgitates it
So many times,
He can't count.

So to love one way,
Is the only thing he knew.

To treat a lady with respect,
Is what he had to do.

You see, every time he sees
Or hears a lady is hurt;
He thinks of his momma.
Inside he weeps when he sees the hurt of anotha.

So he doesn't mean to argue
Or hurt her.
She's his mother.
But there is so much
That she doesn't know.
So much he wishes he could show...

But she's so hurt,
His advances are met with a no.
From different cultures,
On the opposite side of the pole.

This he understands,
So he keeps to himself.
Always wanting to get away;
To avoid any altercation
That would cause a fray.

So all he can say— is...
I love you mommy.

A Window in the Ghetto

After the thunder and lighting,
After the chaos,
There is new life—
And either a rainbow or this:

A grayish blue sky,
Whose horizon is never ending.
In an apartment where the only source of light—
Is television.

This abstract color,
Brings a sullen mood
To the household.
Yet only one view's this phenomenon.

God's beauty is like a blitzkrieg
On the person who realizes it...
And all of it lies in nature.

The trees bask in joy
And dance in happiness,
As the rain filled sky
Waits to unleash another blessing.

A million feet must hide,
Because they do not want to be entrapped
In the minute hurricane.

But when it is over,
They come out to play,
And feast on the residue.

No Way Out

You see the end of the tunnel,
But you can't get out.
You believe in yourself,
Yet you doubt.

You look for answers,
But find no solutions.
You continue to search for the truth—
But no resolution.

What seemed to be reality,
Is now rapidly turning into a dream.
You're stuck in a nightmare,
Replaying scene after scene.

But in your despair,
There is that one thing
Which turns all bad to good.
In all of your confusion,
It is the only thing understood.

Every beginning should have an end;
But this is a cycle
That doesn't want to be shook.
The ones who go through it,
Are often overlooked.

Beautiful Woman

Beautiful Woman.
What a jewel…
God's great tool,
To keep men from playing the fool.
With legs like a stallion,
Eyes of bronze,
Crimson lips,
And a body so voluptuous
That goes far beyond.
Why let a man get you down?
Or make you frown?
When you have a smile,
That can turn any man around.
And one that makes my world
Turn upside down.
Your smile is worth my while…
Beautiful Woman.
Be as beautiful as you are—
Let your light shine brighter than Orion's star,
Beautiful Woman.
No matter which way you put it,
You are so phenomenal…
Someone a man should never forfeit.

Woman- The Greatest Gift

Woman.
God's greatest gift to man;
Besides himself, his son,
And this enormous land.

Soft, sultry, solicit, cocoa skin.
Dark chocolate or vanilla,
Whichever comes from within.

With a presence,
Heavenly and serene as a dove;
She emits celestial emotions,
Those constant and similar to the word love.

Her smell sweeter than Elizabeth Taylor's perfume,
With a body
That has the male hormones in full bloom.

Hmm…
What an unbelievable thing—
I mean what an unbelievable being.

Damn— the words to describe her...
Smooth, slick, thick, some men just don't understand
it.
Fine, hot, wise, with a smile that makes my soul rise.
Persuasive, with a voice that gets her out of
situations—very evasive—
Lips, hips, dips, tastier than a bag of my favorite
potato chips,
Banging louder than a thousand gun clips.

Hmm…
Now I got the word—
Goddess, how could I defer.

It's Crazy
It's crazy how you can't tell a
Girl your true feelings for her…
Cause it makes you whirl and
Twirl, and spins your whole world.

It's crazy how when you see
Two people kiss—and then wonder—
What kind of experience is this?
Is it heavenly bliss? Or could it...
Piss me off to a point of no return,
So that I could not discern,
If I was doing right or wrong?

It's crazy to think about sharing
Your feelings with a woman—and—
Having something like that,
Would it throw me off track?

How 'bout that…
But in fact
It is a beautiful thing.
Love, touch, genius,
Is what a woman brings.

Women, God's greatest gift to man…
Something some men don't understand.
A heavenly treasure, as of right now I may not receive.
Age a hindrance whoa is me—
Now ain't that crazy.

I'm Tired

Fannie Lou Hamer once said,
I'm sick of being sick and tired.
Unfortunately, she's dead.
But her words are still being read.

I'm tired of false tales,
Phony people and propagandas.
I'm tired of people complaining about the government,
While they are on line becoming welfare bystanders.

I'm tired of people who call themselves Christian—
Only open the bible on Sunday;
While they are in church thinking,
"I wish I could get out of here someday."

I'm tired of people celebrating the deaths of those in
great tragedies.
I mean it was a bad thing.
But why don't we celebrate the deaths
Of innocent people, who are shot down by a drug ring?

I'm tired of people being so afraid of death,
That they don't get the big picture.
You may look at me and ask,
"How do you figure?"

My answer is simple …
It is easier than popping a pimple.
I believe in life after death.
I am here and only here to do my best,
So that I can pass the lord's test.

I'm tired
I'm tired
I'm tired…

Lord I'm tired.
Jesus please hurry up and come back.
For those who want to go home—
For the people of which you own—

I'm tired.

Help

When Jesus helped,
He healed, engaged, loved, and protected...
Knowing in the end he would be spat on and dejected.
Seeing years into the future, his words would be neglected.
But still he helped.

For if one could be saved,
By the ounce of compassion he shown and gave—
Fighting for the meek before, during, and after leaving the grave.
You better believe it was worth it to help.

In help: is hope, excess, leisure, and prosperity.
In help: is happiness, excellence, longevity, and probity.
In help: is honor, exaltation, luxury, and proclivity.
In help: is happenstance, exuberance, life, and possibility.

So when I reach my hand, extended, to a longing person;
I smile, because the angels rejoice knowing saving a soul is certain.
We do what we do not for awards, red carpets, or curtains.
But due to love, and the knowledge our brothers and sisters are hurtin.

I challenge you to help, regardless of the cost.

Whether it be physical, financial—regardless of the loss.
Inasmuch as ye did it not to one of the least of these, ye did it not to me—
So says the boss.
Help!

So Many Questions not Enough Answers (A Father's Day Poem)

How do you explain to others,
That the one you call father isn't?
How do you explain to others,
That you want to tell your father
That you love him but can't—
Because the words are not heart felt.
How do you explain to yourself,
Why you don't feel anything…
When he says hello?
How do you fight the anger
When you see your mother struggling,
And your father doesn't seem to help?
Why do I feel this way?
Why do I have these thoughts?
I don't want them.
I shouldn't feel this way.
I hate feeling this way.
But I do.
Why?

LATER TEEN YEARS AND COLLEGIATE LIFE

These were the years that began to mold my creativity in poetry. I began to focus on grammar and word play more. Depiction of vivid images with my words became a signature of mine. I wanted to truly convey what I was feeling. You are getting ready see the world through the eyes of a 16-year-old college freshman, new to independence; growing into a man who would become married at 20, with his first baby girl.

Slain by Beauty

Since the first time I saw you,
The inevitable and irrevocable feeling
Of me being slain by your beauty...
Was untamable.

At the sight of you,
My heart is like the ebb and flow
Of a seismic wave—
Both powerful and unstable.

My mind is trapped in a maze of its own,
Trying to compile and convey
An image that is celestial.

While my body is denied its natural comma,
And my thinking becomes a limbo;
Countless hours are spent,
Of me pondering the woman you are.

The very existence of yours shatters mine.
My thoughts become miniscule,
My surroundings become insignificant,
My body becomes stagnant…
And all there is,
Is you.

Trinity of 4

Every crevice of your lips
Is interwoven with mine.
Tic, toc, tic, toc... tic...toc—
There is a sudden collapse of time.
Thoughts begin to entrap my mind...

The physical becomes the metaphysical.
That night you were no longer a stranger.
The blood rushed to my heart,
And filled all four chambers.

On the trinity of four,
The fourth month and fourth day of 2004;
I felt something that I never felt before.
I felt you and nothing more.

Mi Amor

Mi amor… my God.
This concept of love,
Is such a beautiful thing;
Yet it is not a concept,
Or a feeling, but a decision
To stick through not some,
Not any, but everything.

Mi amor, Mi amor,
The truth is sometimes inside
I feel like I'm about to die—
And inside sometimes I
Scream and cry;
At times I don't even know
Why I try.

But just when I think
I can't…
Love slaps me in the face
And tells me don't ever think like that.

Mi amor, I understand
Why I am so willing to
Endure everything with you.
You are my heart,
My strength, my life,
My everything, and no one can ever fill your shoes.

So, I fight and fight
To be patient and understanding.
Because I know our love is true,

I hold on so long because of you.

Mi amor sometimes
I don't get this idea of love.
It makes me wanna do
Things for you, that I
Would never do for anyone else.
It makes me wanna sacrifice—
Everything, including myself.

Love puts all reason to sleep—
because if it didn't
We wouldn't risk it;
Mi amor you have my heart,
And I want to bring to life all of your wishes.

Made Whole

When it seems that all is going wrong,
I remember that I have you.
When I feel that I am no longer strong,
I think about how your love has brought me through.

My heart
Can no longer contain how I feel.
At times it hurts,
That I can't touch you.
The pain without you is too real.

I reminisce on
The moment we shared our first kiss.
Chills and goose bumps takeover my body,
When I think about the presence I miss.

It feels good when you've found that love
You've been searching for.
Not knowing, that it was only
A few steps from your door.

My heart aches when I think
Of a moment without you.
My love you complete me,
My all and everything I give to you.

A Good Man

I'm of a different seed,
From a different breed,
A hybrid—
There aren't many like me.
So as you can see…
Bitch is not in my vocabulary.
Cursing at my hun is not necessary.
Never putting my hands on you is a definite.
Pleasuring you is my benefit.
I'd never say anything condescending.
I'm gonna give you my all God willing.
A 9 to 5 is a must.
I promise to never violate your trust.
Romance, baby, it ain't a thing;
Flowers, candy, a diamond ring—
Diamonds aren't the only thing forever,
My love is too.
A lady… a queen,
No man could ever turn their back on you.
I'll never hit and run.
I'll commit cuz you're the one.
So ladies don't say there
Aren't any good men;
We're right here.
Ready to show you a love
Like you've never seen before,
And put to sleep all of your
Deepest fears.

Complex yet Simple (For the "intellectual" lover)

My emotions are beginning to seep,
Through every aperture in my skin.
I try to keep my thoughts in cohesion,
But they no longer want to remain within.

This is affinity!
I have already ascertained that this is not love,
Yet it is not infatuation.
What I am unsure of is,
Whether or not this unwavering feeling
Is a part of your mental stimulation?

In my eyes, you are infallible—
In this world, you are indispensable.
I am usually imperturbable.
But as of this moment,
My mind is unstable.
When thinking of you, I am indefatigable!

When I am in your presence,
It is as if you are an apparition.
I am in a stupor; my speech,
Thoughts and being,
Are in sporadic intermission.

The truth is sometimes I feel inept;
You are a jewel that I am undeserving of.
Me thinking that you might have feelings for me,
Is something I should not expect.

As to women,

You are unlike any.
Disparate to all,
Matched by none,
Wanted by all,
Granted to some.

I know my rhetoric
May seem sophisticated.
So let me expound,
And get antiquated.

Roses are Red.
Violets are Blue.
There are a lot of women out here,
But my heart only beats for you.

Emphatic Pleasures

Lips clasped, body heat is felt.
Cells rushing impatiently,
Along conveyor belts.

A moist warm tongue,
Meanders along your
Soft juicy thigh.
Your gluteus maximus quakes,
With every thrust that I apply.

Your sexual lips
Are met by my only;
To ensure
That you are satisfied.
I am here
To make sure that your needs
Are fulfilled,
And that your body is glorified.

As I move my lips
Across your temple,
The foundation starts to shatter.
My kiss—
Sends bolts of electricity
Throughout your body,
And your teeth begin to chatter.

Your lungs
Begin to expand and contract violently,
As my enzymes engulf your chest.
All emotions arise,

That were once put to rest.

Baby oil,
With the aid of my hands,
Lathers your skin.
This moment is about you,
Not me, I plan to relieve
You of all stress and burden.

This moment is only a fraction
Of what is in stored for you.
Whenever you're ready,
I'm willing to indulge you
In emphatic pleasures.
This poem times two.

One Day Imma have to Tell Her

Thoughts of you are constantly
Racking my brain.
When I'm near you,
My composure I try to maintain.

When you smile,
It's like time freezes.
I'm in a dream,
And all life but yours ceases.

Your beauty is like water;
Ever flowing and serene.
You're the kind of woman
I would like to make my queen.

I'm glad I got it off my chest…
My heart and mind can finally rest.
If I did not tell you how I felt,
I would be taking this moment in vain.
Thoughts of what could of and what should of,
Would still remain.

On the real, I'm feelin you,
And in all honesty that's a fact.
P.S. if you're feeling the same,
You know where to find me holla back.

Affinity

Every waking moment, the thought of you
Makes my body tremble.
Every sleepless night,
Your voice gives me solace.
Every day is a blessing,
Because I get another chance at life.
Now every moment is a miracle,
Because I am with you.
Words cannot put forth
The concoction of thoughts,
That reside in my synapse.
Every millisecond I'm with you,
My chambers explode with ferocity.
The magnitude of your presence
Is infinite.
To you I give my heart,
And in return—
All I need is to witness your beauty.

She's Different

Knowing that I've been here before— yet—
Every fear I have goes out the door.
Instantly, I smile when I see her face.
Something about her, makes my heartbeat race.
Hoping she is different from the last.
Already discarding the hurt in my past.

Realizing she is more than a jewel,
Elevating those around her to turn a bad day anew.
Never allowing anything to get her down;
Elegant, too beautiful to frown.
Enticing to others because of her physical;
enchanting to me because her essence can be felt, even when it's distal.

Victim to her kiss and her touch.
Always wanting to give more, cause it's never enough.
Unique, yet sometimes misunderstood.
Gorgeous, because beautiful is not as good.
How could anyone give up on someone, as precious as her?
No one comes close, she's different... wouldn't you concur?

Realizing She's No Longer Here

To think a lot has its benefits.
But to dwell on things,
That you don't wish to think about
Anymore, is painful...
To have an angel
Walk in your life,
Then taken away
Because circumstances cause strife.
Why is it,
That when I thought I had a treasure
It was stripped?
Why is it,
When I finally met
The woman that made me tick,
She was ripped?
Away from me,
From my reality,
Which slightly drove me to insanity.
Sadly, I try to forget.
I still wish, wanting to hold on
But can no longer take it;
Still I never regret.
The repetition of wanting, hoping,
Receiving, and losing,
Has torn away at my being.
The last precious woman I lost,
Was lost for no reason.
And now I go through each and every season:
Summer: seeing her smile, as ice cream
Drops on her chest.
Spring: kissing in the rain,

Realizing she's the best.
Winter: wishing I could hold her for Christmas,
And celebrate the New Year.
I try to, but can't stop my *Fall*: no sleep, no rest,
Longing, wanting, praying—she was near.

Art Thou Thy Brother's Keeper

We've seen Cain kill Abel,
So why do we follow it?
A mother's baby needs food,
And we go on denying it.

We stay worried bout
Jeans and sneakers,
How we gonna get
The latest cells and beepers?
My fault I went too far back...
We stay worried bout
Jeans and sneakers,
How we gonna get
The latest cells and t-shirts?
Children sittin home sayin
Mommy we need you to feed us;
While daddy's out blowin
His money on refer.
Then we look at her,
And say she's a non- achiever.
Cause we too fuckin ignorant
And stupid to believe her.
So goin on welfare,
Is the route that's easier.
She does it, so she won't have to see
Her babies suffer and seizure.
Art thou thy brother's keeper?

The base head on the street,
Been through it all.
Through the ups and downs,

Continuing to fall.
At a soup kitchen, is where
He tries to have a ball.
On lookers ridicule him
And make him small.
But papi could've lost
His job at the mall.
Yet we damage his image cuz
He lives on the park bench—
His headache couldn't be cured by Tylenol.
He comes up to the car asking for a quarter,
And sees you eatin a pizza.
Asks for a dollar,
Then you tell him, Leave me alone,
Nigga I'll holla.
Art thou thy brother's keeper?

Now a hurricane,
That's a bad bitch.
Katrina and Rita validated it.
Pictures of momma cryin cuz
She lost her life and shit.
But you worrying about getting
Your credit consolidated.
Why can't we get
That God put us here for a reason?
To keep each other
From hurtin and bleedin.
But, niggas too worried about
Releasin semen…
Art thou thy brother's keeper?

How can't you be moved,
By seeing a kid watch his momma die?
You can't give a penny?
You'd rather buy
Haagen Dazs.
We look at feed the children
And we ostracize.
Wanting someone else to comply
And compromise.
When will we start to open our eyes?
The roles could easily be reversed,
Surprise—
Now I'm not here to criticize,
Cuz I've done dropped the ball.
At times, I haven't given my all.
But when a nigga disregards the opportunity
To make a difference and rather stay on the corner,
To tell a girl she has no assatol.
How can I look at that nigga,
Without it making my insides crawl?

So after these words that were spitten,
Thoughts that were written,
Shit that I've been in,
Shit that you've been in,
The setting that we live in,
The seats that you sit in,
The knowledge that's been
Received and given…

When I ask you,
Art thou thy brother's keeper?

Save him...
Why do you say,
Don't ask me, ask them?

Poetic Expression

I often question myself
As to why I write. Is it
for the therapy of my mind?
Yes, but also, I can find...
the complexity and simplicity in life.
With this, I sometimes can't control
how I feel about what I see,
or how I feel about what I feel.
And when I can't contain it,
I have to let go, I have to release,
I have to explain it. When I'm done writing
and see what I'm sayin',
it's not done,
cause I have too much remainin'.
This craft, this passion, to create an image with a
pen—
gets me, because sometimes I can't even comprehend.
This may all seem like rubbish,
To the average person.
But to those who have done it,
they know you have to write whether
you're happy or hurtin'.
Of this I'm certain.
To live and die,
Is not a curse but a blessin'.
Too many choices in life,
so we keep on chasin'—
For things we need and want,
Just to be makin' sense out of this place
we were raised in.
Some believe in Allah, others

in Christ and Satan.
All I'm sayin', is thoughts,
thoughts, thoughts, and a pen
can move a nation.

His Story

I saw my brother get whipped,
While my father died.
I saw my wife raped,
Was bound and forced to watch,
Couldn't help but cry.
I saw my child awake to a site,
With no eyes.
I saw my situation and trembled,
But stayed strong knowing God
Would take care of my demise.

I saw a cannon go off...
And kill my kin.
I saw us called in first to begin—
Because Stanley was too soft.
I saw us destroy the "enemy",
And come out with a win.
I saw the recognition never given to us,
Because of our skin.

I saw them call him boy,
Though he was proven to be a man.
I saw him drenched
In the streets of Birmingham;
Beaten until he couldn't stand.
I saw a "peace pipe" being celebrated,
When segregation was delegated.
I saw a man crucified for his words,
When integration was being elevated.

I saw an obstacle overcome,

Then trampled by everyone.
I saw a nigga and a nigger,
And both were his sons.
I saw a life of blood, sweat,
And sacrifice being washed away.
I saw an era of forgetfulness,
Demanding to stay.

I saw a child afraid to walk to school,
For the fear that he might get attacked
By those who thought it wasn't cool.
I saw that child have to live
In an environment so desolate,
Had to grow up without the etiquette,
But still persevered
Because his head was set.

I saw him shot 41 times,
To his one.
I saw him slain...
But it was a crime,
Though he didn't have a gun?
I saw him abused in a cell,
By those sought to protect.
Told not to tell,
In order to watch their neck.

I saw a son become a father,
Because he didn't bother.
I saw a daughter become mother,
Because her uncle told her he loved her.

Through the years I have bled,
But you won't heal me.
All these years you have read,
Several accounts of my story…
The next time you grace me
With something to see,
Will it destroy or bring about our glory.

THIS LOCK   *that key*

I've written about love, sex, hate...
and from different points and vantages.
Thought of cute similes and metaphors to create;
now my source of inspiration sits in bandages.

Some call it writer's block,
others just get stuck.
I can't find the key to the lock,
guess it's just dumb luck.

I was told in nature to have a seat.
Smell the breeze, see the birds, take in the scene;
all the tactics and techniques proved obsolete.
Maybe the key is hidden, lain in a dream?

I see the vibrant gestures of the poets today,
sounds good, but it's definitely not me.
A lot of power, conviction, and movements through
the fray,
this writer performing—definitely cannot be.

On one hand I have the gift to be written.
On the other I have the gift to be risen.
The page and the pen take a seat to the plane of the
living.
The climax and the resolution are too close where's
the division.

That key abodes in a schism.

JADYN

J- Jovial, joyous, jouncing full of jubilation.
Little baby girl,
My greatest manifestation.
Always jolting my stimulation.
Though I grow fatigue,
Never fuming with aggravation.

A- Adoring, adept, adamantly adhesive—

Towards her mother, definitely she is.
Abrasive when hungry,
Abruptly interrupting your sleep,
To put some food in her tummy.

D- Dainty, delightful, dedicated to her dad.
A bit dander,
When she sees food, she wants to have.
Delectable little cheeks,
That leave you in a daze.
A smile, which delivery
You often have to praise.

Y- Young, yawing and yammering,
Yearning for her mother's affection.
At the same time, yielding to daddy's attention.
Looking into their eyes,
Staring at her reflection.
Nodding and smiling with a yes—
Her confirmation.

N- If this were a baby contest,

She'd have a thousand nominations
From the way she's nimble and nibbles.
And of course listening
To her baby conversations,
Cause it gives us the giggles.
The noisy outbursts,
Are usually followed by the nonchalant attitude,
So she can be nurtured.
It was the greatest joy in my life,
To watch her mother birth her.

Stand Still

Hearing her voice feels like a thorn thistle.
You sense the aggravation seeping through your bone
gristle.
Just got off work and don't want no issues,
but she's telling you about dishes and toilet tissue.

So you're frustrated, aggravated, and
discombobulated,
because the situation isn't how you anticipated…
Get over it, cause that's your wife.
Everything sounds like a detriment, not always heaven
sent, mad at the irrelevant,
waste gas on the pavement…
Get over it, cause that's your life.

Yeah it's been a little while, and you have a little
child;
your eyes playing tricks on you because the other lips
didn't smile.
Thinking about things that you normally wouldn't;
seeing a lot of things that you normally should—n't.
Don't let the imagination get over zealous.
That is always dangerous…
Remember who's your wife.

Shhh—and listen now,
remember that in front of the preacher you took vows,
looked at your other hand and said I take thou,
got on your knees and before God did bow...
and at this moment you're seeking a how?

The breeze doesn't always blow in the same direction.
Listen, learn, practice, and heed this lesson.
Lesser men can't conceive or concede this blessing.
So if you choose…Question.

You may: dissect, deject, deflect, offset, eject, or erect
my words—
in your own way.
Still accept, subject, reflect, and respect, what words
she has to convey.
Trust and believe it or not,
when you and her lay.
Ya'll were bound by blood and spirit,
according to what HE say.
Stand Still.

One

We are gathered here today…
were the first words the pastor began to say.
And my thoughts began to lay—
on the layers of my heart.

All nervousness ceased,
anxiety began to decrease;
a smile started to creep,
when I sneaked a peek.

I was holding the hand of an angel;
I knew I was blessed.
The next few moments became unforgettable,
as he proceeded to read the text.

As we turned towards each other,
beautiful wasn't strong enough.
I could only think to call you perfect,
because you have been perfect for me,
since we fell in love.

As I gazed into your eyes,
I saw you swell with tears.
I couldn't cry.
It felt too good, thinking about being with you for the
rest of our years.

As we reached the I do's—
I realized that it wasn't for me or you.
It was us and we, never to be undone.

Our souls, our bodies, our love, was established as one.

She is Not Just Any She

She is the love and the kiss,
That I wait and long for.
She is the woman, the confidant that I miss;
Yearning to see her beautiful smile more and more.

She is the physical presence,
That causes my physical to be shaken.
She is indeed that essence,
That has my soul taken.

She is the water I drink,
Both refreshing and pure.
She is the thought that allows me to think,
The steadfast allowing me to endure.

She is not just any she.
No...
For her to be any,
There would have to be many;
But there are none that can compare.

She is unlike any other.
She is that ever burning fire.
She is no ordinary she—
In fact, she is not called by she.
My Darling, My Lady, My Love,
My Desire.

If It Were Not For The Thin

How can I say I love you?
When there aren't any memories,
To show what we've gone through.

If there wasn't a time that we frowned,
What would we learn from?
How could we get past
The tribulation now?

Though there are many times of joy,
The truth is there are a lot of times we hurt,
Our passion becomes coy.

If it were not for the thin,
We wouldn't exist
To engage in each other;
When other lovers would be amiss.

See without the thin,
There would be no thick.
The downs is all
The ammunition I need,
To make our relationship stick.

There is no happiness,
Without pain.
There is no Abel,
Without Cain.

When I said I love you,
It was thick.

And now that it's thin,
My love still won't shift.

All that thin is,
Is a way for me
To figure out how to love you better—
So that the thick,
Will eventually stay forever.

Cherish Her (Remember)

Remember the first time you told her your name.
It was nerve racking; your body became a little lame.

And the first time you kissed; how your heart skipped
a beat.
The softness of her lips, and how you couldn't sleep.

Making love for the first time, the passion was
overwhelming.
Saying I love you for the first time, you couldn't keep
the tears from swelling.

Remember when you proposed, and you couldn't stop
shaking.
You choked up and felt froze, but your ring was still
taken.

Remember when you held her hand, and glanced into
her eyes.
You became one, exploding with joy at the sight of
your wife.

Treat her with respect, and cherish her as much as you
can.
Make sure you sleep with no regret, thinking of how to
make your love expand.

While you remember the past, take care of her now.
Make these memories memorable, because tomorrow
isn't a vow.

Sleepwalking

I sleep in the real world more often than naught,
though I traverse the two planes profoundly at night.
Journey with me as I stimulate your thoughts,
see clearly for perception at times deems light.

Goddesses don't walk among men.
Good fruit doesn't bear on worn trees.
When my queen lies down in my den,
a man I cannot be.

The beast must be contained;
supernatural creatures don't dwell in reality.
I still crave for affection in vain,
even Earth senses the gravity.

My Love, My Heart, My Wife.
As you slumber I wonder,
who bestowed such grace to my life?
Your beauty causes my heart to thunder.

Do understand I'm asleep yet awake.
My Lady's magnificence distorts my vision.
Altered is my present state;
reflected is my position.

The womb-man that birthed my joy,
does rest more peaceful than ever.
More serenity and elegance than God himself can
employ,
there is no greater gift than this endeavor.

Blessed am I,
to behold this glorious master piece;
fortunate are these eyes,
to watch an angel put together so masterfully.

Oblivious and cognizant of the sensation;
stunned and stirred by the divination.

Witness this majestic scene…
When she sleeps, I dream.

About the Author

Brooklyn native Gnatee Doe, is a poet, author, motivational speaker, police officer, and U.S. Army sergeant who currently lives in Daytona Beach, Florida. Though he graduated with a bachelor's of science degree in Criminal Justice from the great Bethune-Cookman University, his passion has always resided in his minor in English.

In addition to studying the craft of writing, he also engages in outreach by speaking with at risk youth and organizing community events. Since the age of ten, he has found the pen to be the most effective way to express his perspective of life.

Instagram: @takeawalkwithme.3

Instagram: @themotivationmagnet

Twitter: @GnateeDoe

LinkedIn: Gnatee Doe

I thank you for allowing me to share a piece of myself with you. This anthology has been a long time coming, and it is a phenomenal feeling to open up my work to the world. I leave you guys with a preview from my upcoming anthology, *Leave on E: Poems of Power, Passion, Purpose and Perspective*. This piece entitled "I Jumped", was inspired by Steve Harvey. I wrote it, while listening to a moment he shared with his audience during a Family Feud taping. He spoke about their gifts and what it takes to be successful.

I Jumped

I jumped, no reserve;

Saw 10,000 falling.

Looked up, counted to 5;

Saw 10,000 calling.

Saw mine; met it with a smile,

Then started sprawling.

Pop cord, no discord;

Stood up—got to hauling.